Urban Snow

I dont want to die in the urban snow

•

I dont want to die in the urban snow
Far from the dark orange heart of the wood

•

I hear two voices coming up through the floor,
I dont want to die in the urban snow
Far from the dark orange heart of the wood

•

I hear two voices coming up through the floor
I dont want to die in the urban snow
Far from the dark orange heart of the wood
Its muse making lazy figure eights in the ether

•

I am made uneasy by crumpled brown paper bags
I hear two voices coming up through the floor
I dont want to die in the urban snow
Far from the heart of the dark orange wood
Its muse making lazy figure eights in the ether

•

I am made uneasy by crumpled brown paper bags,
I hear two voices coming up through the floor;
I dont want to die in the urban snow
Far from the heart of the dark orange wood,
Its muse making lazy figure eights in the ether
Safe in the knowledge that I am on another continent

•

My lethal hair hangs over my forehead now,
I am made uneasy by crumpled brown paper bags,
I hear two voices coming up through the floor;
I don't want to die in the urban snow
Far from the dark orange heart of the wood,
Its muse forming lazy figure eights in the ether,
Safe in the knowledge that I am on another continent.

URBAN SNOW

George Bowering

Talonbooks   •   Vancouver   •   1991

published with the assistance of the Canada Council

Talonbooks
201 / 1019 East Cordova Street
Vancouver, British Columbia
Canada, V6A 1M8

Typeset in Garamond Book and Bookman Medium by Pièce de Résistance Ltée.
Printed and bound in Canada by Hignell Printing Ltd.

First printing: January 1992

Acknowledgements: The Bastard Press, Imprimerie Dromadaire, The Malahat Review, Mattoid (Australia), Nexus, Poetry Canada Review, Quarry, Span (New Zealand), Talonbooks, The Toronto Star Magazine, University of Toronto Review, West Coast Cards, and various CBC programmes.

Canadian Cataloguing in Publication Data

Bowering, George, 1935-
    Urban snow

        Poems.
        ISBN 0-88922-305-X

        I. Title.
PS8503.0875U7 1992   C811'.54   C92-091068-8
PR9199.B69U7 1992

CONTENTS

This book is for Red Lane, bp nichol, Gwen MacEwen and Robert Duncan, Joel Oppenheimer and George Butterick

Who Cares

It is with your eyes
you see your eyes
sunk deeper yet into your head.

It's so long since you last said
never give up you cant remember
ever saying it.

Who cares, if dying is after you
there's nowhere you can go to hide,
no deep recess inside.

Unser Karl

If you were an enemy of poetry and it was morning the worst thing you could see would be Karl Siegler's smile.

I like Karl Siegler's smile; it generally signals a necessary irony about a recent meeting with a government bureaucrat.

Sometimes when you are looking at Karl Siegler's smile you know that out of sight behind it isnt so hot.

Actually, Karl Siegler's smile is only half there; the other half will be brought out when your manuscript is perfect.

If you saw Karl Siegler's smile on the front of the mayor's face you would go and sell all your furniture.

I have to stop writing this—the birds are filling my tree with high noise; six of them could perch on Karl Siegler's smile.

Silver in the Silver Sun

John Newlove and I have shared a writing career gone off in two directions.

I always liked writing his poems and could hardly wait for them to be published so I could read them for the first time.

He has taught me all I know about poetry, but I always knew it before he did.

Nobody knows better than John Newlove how to make a line and how to make a stanza and I have always been proud of them.

John and I have never collaborated on a poem, but there isnt one really good one that doesnt have both our hands in it.

It always embarrasses me to review a book of Newlove's because I know I am just stating his opinion.

I wish I could be there at his fiftieth birthday celebration, but then he would have to be here writing this.

I hope we have another fifty years in us, but if we dont I hope we have time for a glass of Irish whiskey. A double.

Canada Puzzle

When I was a little kid fifteen miles from the border I got a neat Christmas present. It was a jigsaw puzzle map of Canada.

I put it together and took it apart, over and over. It was not a game; it was a puzzle.

I got really good at it. I could put Canada together upside down. I could do it in the dark.

Then as often happens I lost a piece. I did what people always do when a jigsaw piece goes missing.

I threw the whole thing out.

Leaves Flipping

The leaves flipping green and silver in the wind

Moon eye daughters bend necks, looking at
the leaves flipping green and silver in the wind

Moon eye daughters bend necks, looking at
the leaves flipping green and silver in the wind
just this side of South Dakota, 1948

Say welcome great baseball season, give us all
moon eye daughters bending necks, looking at
the leaves flipping green and silver in the wind
just this side of South Dakota, 1948

Say welcome great baseball season, give us please
moon daughters, bend necks, looking at
the leaves flipping green and silver in the wind
just this side of South Dakota, 1948,
a peaceful objective, a family gathering, rain barrel

She sits carelessly in a white painted iron chair,
says welcome great baseball season, give us all
moon daughters, bend long necks, looking at
the leaves flipping green and silver in the wind
just this side of South Dakota, 1948,
a peaceful objective, a family gathering, rain barrel

She sits carelessly in the white painted iron chair,
says welcome great baseball season, give us both
moon daughters, bend long necks, looking at
the leaves flipping green and silver in the wind
just this side of South Dakota, 1948,
a peaceful objective, a family gathering, rain barrel,
dust rising behind a coupé getting larger as it arrives.

Late Goddess

Isis
Isntisnt

Acute

To my left
at the paper on Hugh MacLennan
my wife sleeps,
her arms
folded.

Old time
Eastern Canadian Literature
flickers into slight life
among Vancouver Island
trees.

But my wife
doesnt know this, she is
I hope dreaming
of a west coast
fiction.

One solitude
is hers, lucky auditor.
I have to write my own
with this un-
referential pen

looking every minute
at my watch that will
end the hour
she nods
right through.

Dear David McFadden

All the coincidences that have
lighted up the dark stretches of your life?

I arranged them all,
down to the last detail.

If you were just thinking the same thing,
now you know why.

An Epithalian Draft For Bev & Dwight

We saw bright sun
on the backs of goldfish,
on the top of Nitobe Gardiner,
on the cedar bark the trees are still using.

      Beverly Matsu
      is a very strong swimmer,
      she ascends from a long line of fisherfolk,
      she knows all there is to know about poetry.

"It is not
      raining in" Vancouver.

"Love is understanding the weather."

All we need is a neat oboe,
a bird flying out of its little bell,
yes then
he would dance in his nuptial shoes
& Bev would say yet again, "Right, Dwight."

A soul station, a brand new frequency, a white rabbit, Akemi
in our ears.

      Those gold fish
      have wings, they have flown
      like all of us, sharing the gods
      in the air, drinking something like music
      to this groom, this more fair.

                  (Aug. 1986)

Twenty

It doesnt matter whether you're twenty or fifty
when you're pissing on the ground
under the stars
you're connected with
who cares, this has been life,
here it comes dark, roiling silently, eternity

as long as you have your feet wide apart
and no one is pissing too close to you
especially on rocks, there it goes
your last pure intention
how sweet that was, and you look for it
in vain in your offspring

they have another idea, which does not even
recognize eternity, they worship
their own good looks, they never stop
to consider the person from whom the liquid is stolen
it is dark out, there are people
pissing in headlights now
and some are your relatives

you are not twenty, though if you went
to where you were twenty
say up the hill below the umbrella tree
in the dark and opened your modern pants
and pissed on the sloping ground
where there were no family around
you would keep wetting the ground
just out of your adolescence

No Meeting

We will go down with all of them,
slaves of love, slaves of freedom,
losers at last, save that woman
who told me she will win
by jumping off the ferry. Her parents too
leaving her and their bright world,
as are mine, as are yours, neither
jumping, one lying unable to turn, the other
buying a new Toyota, to go where?

Slaves of freedom, slaves of fury,
we will go away where they went,
but not as our grandparents thought they knew
toward a meeting with them again.
We feel their going before they are gone
and our own while there is time,
our life an old car gone off the road,
a failure of nerve. It will be a car ferry.
Will she walk on, a hobbling pedestrian?

First Born

First I was born,
then I fell in love.

My mother says I was
a difficult birth, someone

could have died. When
I fell in love, or shortly after

I wanted to slit my throat
or more likely lie down

and go away, back
where I came from.

(Auckland, July, 1988)

Jodine

Girls & even women
in small Canadian towns
belong to teams, they wear
team jackets
with their names on their upper arms.

In the airport I just saw Jodine,
who reminded me of Leanne.
Their uncle Vern used to wear
a bowling shirt
with his name stitched over a pocket.

I bought Vern's shirt years ago
in a Sally Ann, but then
I hardly ever wore it, not
because of my name, but because
the buttons came off.

I'm from a small Canadian town,
where we survived
on spurious connections, just like
Jodine. Imagine seeing you here
she said every time.

Here in Attachment

I cant help it, I still
panic when I notice the sun's
going down. Going down

what will prevent its continuing
to fall, down, to grow
smaller, unseen as it does?

Who will come to help us, I say
save us, are we all together
here in attachment, or just

dying in a multitude, bereft.
In the morning I am never there
to see its returning, and at noon

I have forgotten again, as we must
forget the dreams in which we perish
to keep on living.

Death

I'm going to write a poem about life & death, I said,
but mostly about death. But you are always doing that, said D,
your last poem was about death. The poem before that one was
about death. In fact if you looked at all your writing, especially
the poems, you would find pretty near nothing but death. A lot
of the time you seem to be laughing about it, but that doesnt
fool anyone.

Yes, but this time I am going to make it a real poem about life
but mainly death, I'll grant you that. None of that lacy Rilke
death, none of that ho ho Vonnegut death. I mean real death
or I should say real thinking about death. For instance? asked
D. Well, for instance, take the way you feel like how awful it
will be when you cant put an arm around a waist, long arm the
way it is just made to snake around a perfect waist, & there
is that swelling out of hip upon which it is natural to rest
an arm. How wonderful, and how terrible not to be able to look
forward to that ever again.

You see? said D, you announce that you are going to say something
straight about death, and there you are talking about life,
as far as I can see. That's just my point, I said. Death will be
horrible because it wont have anything of life in it, no matter
how many fancypants graduate students have told me that you cant
really submerge yourself in life unless you are fully conscious
of your death. They have all been reading Albert Camus lately,
& they are so much wiser than I am.

I suppose you are using all the things I have been saying as
part of your poem, said D. Of course, I said. You are to this poem
as a swelling out of lovely hip is to an arm that has snaked
around a dear waist.

Just then I realized that I had made D up in my imagination, &
now there was no D at all, & I had to forget about writing
another poem about life & death but especially about death,
especially about death from a straight point of view, because
M came into the room while I was typing & had a persistent gripe
about C, & no matter how interrupted I managed to make myself
look on the chair in front of the keyboard, M just kept on &
on till the poem had followed D to some place we will never find
the way to.

Endless Vees

Why, I said to Bob in Ottawa,
worry about origins?
We're here, arent we?

Above the city this morning
endless vees of Canadas
pointing north. I guess it was north;
you can never tell in Ontario.

After we landed in Toronto
a brown rabbit scampered
over the grass, away from our 727.

I'm just on my way home.
Right now I'm flying over
the town where I was born.

The girl in the short skirt
with chubby legs is telling
seat 29F how much she loves
living in Ottawa at last.

Found in the Endpapers of a Larry Eigner Book

When he said
      Let there be light

where were the eyes
      to gather it?

He saw that it was good,
      and went on,

a super solipsist
      at the beginning.

But then why
      did he say it?

Grizzle Boy

How I miss my father,
crumbling crackers into tomato soup.
I see him doing that,
goofy smile and stern forehead,

I must have been a watching boy
all the time, to save up
all those scenes, my Dad
and me, mountaintop, kitchen.

How can I miss a man
younger than I am now, grey whiskers?
Oh, you should see him
the way he stands like James Joyce

and him just an Okanagan boy,
thinking of basketball, not me.
I miss him fully, and long ago
we all thought we'd meet again.

Fall Notes

When in November
            the leaves fall
off the little
            maple tree
they are replaced
            by twenty-two
chickadees.

                    •

        Hello,
I hear you,
            breakfast is
coming,
            friends,
my singing
            leaves.

                    •

[Are they there because
they feel love leaking
out of the house?

Or are they just birds, song
we know from childhood,
in a little tree now,

somewhere else
in minutes?]

My Family's All In Bed

I'm up
against the silences to come   .

They keep telling me to talk more,
write less—

but I cant figure this out, I
will be doing neither
soon enough   .

      And think
when the ears that hear me talk are dead
I'm done forever
talking   .

      But someone,
dear descendent,
might read a page out loud
in the twenty-first century,
her familiar time—

and there I'll be (no book, etc.)
where neither you nor I can hear me   .

But closing the book, someone
will close my words on each other,

maybe these I'm writing in a lorn kitchen,
dark January outside,
a lot of silence in this place   .

The Drift

In Canada, he said, you have
a nuclear winter every year,
but the sun always, he said,
comes back, and you have
another wheat harvest.

                                The gift,
I figure, of the magi.

You will follow a star
if there is no sun. A moth
will aspire to Venus
if he cant find a flame.

So Christmas. It comes to Flin Flon
when Flin Flon, I mean for example,
needs it. A Canadian winter,
the one they show me on billboards,
is no idyl, the god of snow
does not fiddle, no cow I know
can jump from the foothills
over the moon.

2.

This is the month, and this
the happy morn, he said. Yes
and the unhappy are filled
with jubilation. It depends

like a full stocking off a fireplace
mantle, it depends. Do you see
the death of winter born
with the deepest December snow?

Do you see that billboard,
deep tire tracks in the white,
a Canadian winter—it's
expensive. We know who's filled

with jubilation. Every winter
is new and every midnight is clear,
and someone has to pay
for those long tall magnesium candles

cuddled in their electronic silos,
round yon virgin, under the drift
of dry snow, belly deep in
the collected blood of the roast lamb.

3.

And then, they said, no spirit can walk abroad,
Flin Flon, hunkered at our heart, is sure,
its fires burn friendly molecules, some god
we celebrate clenches us, like a young woman
in a Japanese car, before the heater kicks in.

The night is wholesome, no planets strike.
Our friendly fire burns till dawn,
while north of us the Dew Line rots away.

No fairy takes, nor witch has power to charm,
so sacred is the time, so gracious,
so forgetful are we, so loud did Santa
roar from his disguised motor
on the bare pavement, in the mall.

She's a schoolteacher, that's why
she's in that Japanese car. It is
almost new. It is driving along
one of the cross-hairs in a distant scope,
but she doesn't know that.

She thinks it is the invisible
Saskatchewan border. She can see lines of lights
that are winter roofs
in Manitoba.

4.

What harvest?
What gift?
Who magi?

In a drear-nighted December, he said,
too happy, happy tree,
your branches dont remember
their green felicity.

The tree, the tree, the Christmas
tree cut down dead, Jesus
come down, the old decorations
go back up, the star no sun on top.

The tree, dying slowly, like a world,
is covered with shiny
petroleum products, magic for the very young,
goodbye for a pine
that never will be.

This the happy never morn,
they'll chuck him over the fence,
brown in the back lane, crisp
in the wet snow; never count the rings,
his age, never see
the invisible god, never evergreen.

5.

If winter comes, he might say,
spring can be so far behind,
she'll never catch up.

If winter comes upon a midnight
new and clear, even Mr. Flin Flon
will not have time

to remember Satan, on his motor,
on the soft pavement, in the mall,
waving his bright red arm
at them all.

A sad song, a carol
at every doorstep.
We do need the time, this dark afternoon,
to sleep in earthly peace.

We do need you, sleeping child,
we do need you, soil asleep
beneath a brittle snow.

We do need you, poets of the seed,
stacked in the warm shed,
waiting for an ancient sun.

We need you, too, you unnameable,
blow the flame off your candles,
climb out of that warm concrete hole,
put your heart's gloves on,

give us two hands, help us
push this little Japanese car
out of the drift.

BERLIN

Wish I Were

I keep wishing
I were home
so I could talk about
how much I enjoyed Europe

wish I were home
where all my paper is
so I wouldnt have to
scratch out a poem in a restaurant
on a subscription form
ripped from a Canadian magazine.

You wish I would say
I feel too far away from you
and I thought I did
wishing I was home
so you could read the poem.

Birds In The Tiergarten

They can fly over the graffiti wall
any time they want to
but I looked at it and over it
for one hour and not one
did it
        though I saw a B737
tilt a wing over there
to land over here.

Now the Berliners
have always loved dressing up
and hunting in their woods
but those are not bird guns
the gents on the towers carry.

When you wave at them
they look but they dont wave back.

In the Tiergarten the long-necked doves
perch low in the nearly bare trees
exchanging a few words
and refusing to let you get away
with a mere sonnet.

Every Night

The nights are lonely, yes
long and alone, no
quibbles in the kitchen,
no cats to kick
out of the way.

Berlin, he said
is a long Burnaby, the days
are filled with business
called learning.

Reaching, a little, touching
maybe, but his grasp
every night is the German
TV knob; he settles and watches
two worlds speaking one language
he does not know.

No hip to touch on the way
by to get another coffee,
no hair to tousle at bedtime,
no bright and then faltering
piano, only
the bored voice of a socialist
news reader.

The Difference

Today on East German TV
I heard a musician explain
the difference betwen jazz and funk

so dont tell *me*
there's no progress in the arts.

Personal Narrative

When I visited West Germany in 1966
the war-wounded were everywhere,
middle-aged fractional men,
visible men with arms gone, lopsided in jackets,
visible men twirling along park trails on wooden crutches,
visible men with ears gone, whole sides of faces
like 1945 photos of Berlin rubble.

Now they are seldom seen, nineteen years later,
lonelier in the city for their time,
hanging on surrounded by children with green hair,
the odd old man negotiating a mall
in his motorized tricycle,
and the little countrified guy in black,
looks like a 1930 peasant from the east.

He's kneeling on his stumps
in front of a gaudy department store
built since he last saw his feet,
he's turning the handle of an old box organ,
looks as if he's had it forty years.

Sure, I drop some pocket coins into his hat,
it's easier on you now, I mean now
I'm middle-aged, and there are
so few of these fellows around.

Hitler's Bunker

Hitler's bunker is still under Berlin.
It was too massive to destroy. It's
still there, an idea
camouflaged by earth.

I hear the rumble of the subway
every seven minutes, under
Berlin, below my window.
History moves a lot slower.

Did Herr Hitler ride the subway
once in a while, did he
sit avoiding the eyes
of the young person across the car?

Could he hear the underground
from his bunker? Do little people
in the Tiergarten think of the invisible
architecture they walk over?

Above all, I guess I mean
is there an underlying continuity
in the city's story, an archaeology
hostile to the orderly shovel?

To Live In

Why should I tell you
what it's like, when I
have trouble with
what it is?

        A stark
pain in my chest, boring
buildings with no history,
I came nine thousand miles
for a city younger than my own.

It's like, well you know
when your ears are stuffed
and you dont mind
missing the sounds, it's the
world next to you you wish
you could get clear.

Dear Hitler, you say,
if you werent dead I'd kill you,
you took away Berlin
for my lifetime.

You left me a three-story building
thrown together
with a bathroom fixture store
at street level.

Ku'damm Eck

Those werent crazy eyes you saw on the street,
those were lonely eyes.

There was a thick moving crowd
for her too, she lives here,
she's a Berliner

just as you are, she's downtown
for no better reason than you are.

Commonwealth Conference, Jagdschloss Glienicke

This side of the narrow water we
sit in a hunting lodge listening
to endless lectures on distant authors
we have never got round to reading.

That side of the narrow water
they stand behind their windows
up a gun tower above a wall
no one could possibly reach.

We have to wait a certain while
for coffee and our cigarettes. They
can smoke all they like. We will
never agree on freedom and geography,

never trade "rare insights"
during any question period you know about.

(1985)

On The Picadilly Tube

On the Picadilly tube
(ON a tube? what country is this?)
above ground from Heathrow
he held a suitcase and a shoulder bag
(nice leather, Mon) in front of him
& came one half inch (they still use
Imperial measures over here)
from throwing up in the crowd,
winter jackets, blue jeans.

•

A half-pint (see above) of bitter
in the Sail and Steam,
Sixties music cutting through cigarette smoke,
made him feel better
(he was awake enough to rime);
spaghetti puttanesca (or some such spelling)
made him feel Roman.

•

Nearly puked—that was
(pardon me) the second time in two weeks.
He knows what goes into a stomach
& what should. A bag of salt & vinegar crisps
out of a machine—20 p.

•

His friend since childhood is in the little shower
after midnight (somewhere on the slippery surface
of the Globe), this little hotel
(less than an everywhere, he can tell you)
on Ebury Street, trying to find
the warm water. Earlier
he showed his friend the dark Thames.

•

Many the poet's
chucked his colonial dinner
from that bridge.

Circle Line Hokku

I saw Africans
in London

baffled
in the Underground.

Music In The Park

Ambient auto traffic outside our heads,
we dont register which way the noise comes,
till it stops, and we hear above us
birds in the trees, singing every jump from branch to branch,
announcing the day through, and beneath them now

an outdoor saxophone, a tenor
breath through warm brass, its own birds gaining strength,
a long curious honk, a melody
fell off a table in a cubic city too far back east.

     This is summer in Vancouver,
     a city like others on the coast of Australia.

     Or maybe it's more accurate
     to say the west edge of Canada.

You know the voices of little kids in the park?
It doesnt matter what they're playing,
could be twig-ball, throw the doll, get tired, fall down.

     Vancouver
     is an Australian kind of town.

     Citizens here do everything outdoors.
     Chances are they will never look like Australians,

     those people with universal suntan,
     but you'll blame the cloud-cover, not the skin.

     Vancouver people play tennis at Christmas,
     go swimming New Year's Day.

     They read light fiction on the patio,
     they cook moussaka in the street,

     they've been known to procreate on every beach
     and soccer pitch around the lower mainland.

2.

Sometimes it rains
(no)
in Vancouver.

What do you get
after two days of rain in Vancouver?

Monday.

Saturday morning in any neighbourhood
you see a front door opening.

Two little kids in yellow slickers,
their smiling mother behind them

sending them out
to play in the rain.

3.

In Kerrisdale a crow caws. Below his tall dark roost
bowling balls clack, friendly encouraging voices speak for

The Kerrisdale Lawn Bowling Club. Visitors welcome.
They used to wear pure white outfits, these senior folk, let's say.
All the accents used to be British.
Now it's golf hats and checkered double-knits.

A duffer shouts quietly:
"Just a little wider, Jack!"

No great European history is being decided here.
Still it is odd to hear geezers with Canadian accents
on the rolled grass.

Under huge cedars and maples the old guys and their widows
bend carefully. After they release the eccentric ball
they use minimal body English.

The loudest sound is the veteran human voice,
and the most frequent question is:
"What end is this?"

It is a question any welcome visitor might ponder, sitting there in the shade,
sitting there in a body that has itself been around.
A mile or two away, a block behind glossy Granville Street,
gentle lawn bowlers labour under a cruel sign that proclaims in giant letters:
TERMINAL CITY LAWN BOWLING CLUB.

4.

But summer keeps coming around, keeps coming around,
and when you're in it it seems to be there always,
and life is long, isnt it? Life is long,
isnt it?

In Carnarvon Park the kindergarten kids are learning high jump.
In kindergarten the tiny girls and stubby boys still play together.
The bar isnt very high, if you're looking down at it.
The tiny girl starts a long way back and runs and runs and runs and runs,
and she runs and runs and runs,
and this is not a metaphor for life at all, she is just running and running,
and now she is staggering a little, and when she gets to the bar
she hasnt got anything left, some athlete, she just falls across the bar.

                    The sax
                    o phone
                    honks &
                    honks &
                     stops
                       •

Her teacher will say Nice try, Michelle, you're a good runner,
preparing her for a life that resembles a grassy park in June.

49

Neither of them knows there's a man in a made-to-measure blue suit
sitting at a white telephone behind some black-tinted windows
high in grey cement downtown;
                              he is not interested in Carnarvon Park.
Dont get him wrong, he likes green as much as the next man.
But he keeps in shape in a windowless room he can write off
as an expense.

5.

        Vancouver is just about surrounded by other communities
speckled with parks. Richmond was built on top of what used to be
the best vegetable-growing soil in the world, so its playing fields are
as green as can be. In Surrey the deer and coyotes and bears step by
night from woods onto playing fields. On the North Shore they have
built a park where Malcolm Lowry wrote about his natural paradise.
There is a public toilet now where there was once the Forest Path
to the Spring.
        But forget the suburbs. In Vancouver alone there are 141 parks
with a total of just under three thousand acres under Park Board con-
trol, as they say. That works out, you might be astonished to learn,
to one acre for every 141 people in Vancouver. Or three thousand
to a park. Just enough room for everyone to practice a little *Tai Chi*,
like the old women in black pajamas at Templeton Park in the east end.

6.

An aluminum baseball bat
clinks.

A grown up coach
complains
encouragingly.

In the old black and white movies, the boys playing baseball in the dirt were called Tony, Mike and Johnny. Now on the Versailles-like lawn of Memorial Park West, just off Dunbar Street, the ten-year-olds are Anthony, Michael and Jonathan —all of them younger brothers of Pony-Leaguers named Jason. There are new Volvos and BMW's lined up around the park, and a large new sign attached to the fence behind first base:

Parks by-law prohibits the leaving of dog defecation in any park. In the interest of public hygeine, please remove your dog's defecation & help keep this park clean. Failure to comply will result in a $50 fine.

Hark, hark!

The forgotten tenor horn is oops, sudden lee a lick . . .

The way these kids look and the way they are playing is pure prose.

Their gloves are too big for their hands. Their hats have holes in the back and they are too big for their hairy heads. They carry advertisements on their backs. Legion #142 is beatint Stong's Meats 19-0.

Behind the little bank of bleachers there are children racing their dirt bikes where there isnt a sign of dirt, in patterns created by the flick of a brain, a flick of the wrist. In front of the little bleachers there are eighteen boys striving without a smile, under the paternalistic advice of volunteer grown-ups: "Now *that's* the way to swing that bat, Simon." Simon has just struck out on three swings.

A father in the bleachers says a lot of kids never had it so good. They got nice green grass, free uniforms, umpires, coaches helping them. Lots of kids never had the opportunity.

•

Fun in Little League?

—Well, it's kind of hard
but not too hard.

You have to get used to your glove.
The ball has to be nice and hard.

You learn to throw.
You learn to catch.

And you bat.

7.

For a few hours,
              for a summer,
                        we think we know them,
these young men in three-coloured caps,
                        playing

the game of boyhood,
                              brief in our eyes.
Do they play for us,
                              or are they performing
the ancient demands of their decorated bodies?

They wear their names on their backs.
but they wear costumes designed a century past,
of gentlemen met of a Sunday on the grass.

S. SAX
oh phone!

TOWARD THE END OF THE NINETEENTH CENTURY,
ANOTHER EFFORT TO IMPROVE URBAN ENVIRONMENT
EMERGED FROM THE RECOGNITION OF THE NEED FOR
RECREATION. PARKS WERE DEVELOPED TO PROVIDE
VISUAL RELIEF AND PLACES FOR HEALTHFUL PLAY OR
RELAXATION. LATER, PLAYGROUNDS WERE CARVED OUT
IN CONGESTED AREAS, AND FACILITIES FOR GAMES AND
SPORTS WERE ESTABLISHED NOT ONLY FOR CHILDREN BUT
ALSO FOR ADULTS, WHOSE WORKDAYS GRADUALLY
SHORTENED.

The white ball acts upon them as a stone in a pool.
They run, they bend, they leap, they fall
to the patchy green carpet,
walled away from the forest city.

The eye up high for a moment catches
a soft human Diamond,
                              a star
twinkt in a moment by the hurl, the ex-
stacy of the thing among them.

•

**Vancouver is one hundred years old. Wasnt Vancouver lucky
to get started just when they invented city parks?**

**Because those cedar-covered mountains
will have to go, buddy.**

•

Diamonds,
             this green Diamond at Little Mountain, at
Queen Elizabeth Park,
where these, younger than we, leap and run and fall
like our older brothers,
                         where we shout inanities
from our high wall,
                     our wit echoes loudly
off the right field fence.

                         This is not
poetry,
         neither is it play;
                             it is life
whether you like it or not,
                             money
changes hands,
                 the sun goes purple and gold
behind the trees,
                   the lights come on bright,
the ball is white,
                     and someone
has to pay for it.

                    8.

                    (a sweet piano threw its notes
                    among the branches, birds shifted
                    their weight, a monk supreme
                    lifted his cowl, a breeze grew
                    something like love)

Arbutus
Park
Camosun
Park
Connaught
Park
Cradle of the Cosmic League
Hastings Community
Park
Kitsilano
Park
Locarno
Park
When the Indians had it they called it
Eyalmu
That meant
Nice Park

                      (the piano
                      quit

                      ting)

When people in Europe set up gardens with vine-covered walls around them, they were making images of Eden, yes. And when city planners in Canada set aside space for green parks, they illustrate our desire for innocence made public. Yes, young parents and doting grandparents feel a duty to take their little children to the park. That's why dog defecation is such a problem; you didnt have to watch where you were sitting down in Eden.

Little League retains a bit of innocence, even when a businessparent in the bleachers requests of his son Jonathan at the plate a greater degree of aggressivity, to smack that apple. Hmm.

But a few blocks north, at Chaldecott Park, the organized late teenagers are playing. Dunbar against the Royals.

These boys look like men at a distance.
They hardly ever drop the ball.
They dont yell "Nice try!"

They holler "Take this guy out!"
They are testing their narcissisitic male aggression.
They have sweaty hair spilling from their baseball caps.
Their coaches are older.
Their coaches have wide asses,
gruffy voices,
real rawbone pose.

Did he who made the lamb make thee?

> A brown truck passes,
> making no music but
> a grind of post-edenic
> noise.

Be fair, you tell yourself. This game is probably fun to play.
This cheesy machismo is probably a necessary part
of whatever the psychologists call growing up now.

But it's not much fun to watch.
Across the street is a little forest, a cleared path wandering through.
It is cool in there. It is soothing.
In there you dont have a clue how old you are now.

9.

This is a highly cultured forest that rings the University of British Columbia, the kind of sylvan respite through which you should walk slowly, with twenty-four lines of Wordsworth snaking their way without interruption through your shaded mind. On its edge, striving to look more simple than its expensive amenities really are, is one of those imitation-British private schools for boys. St. George's. Not a dragon in sight. Here as elsewhere in what is called after all *British* Columbia, they essay that game that not only builds but also proves character—Cricket.

(Singing: all together—)
*And did those feet
in ancient time* . . .

56

It is a fascinating game, in which people stand still, generally, walk when they can, reluctantly run when they must, and endeavour not to perspire. It was invented to show naked people in the stations of the Empire that Englishmen, through their proven will, are immune to anything nature can throw at them.

No sax, please,
we're British.

So there are no high-fives in this game.
The game isnt over till the last man's out
in the mid-day sun,
and that could be days from now.

This is what the grassy parks are for. The streets may be there to move commerce, empirical grids of referential realism. The park is arbitrary, a kind of game itself. And the game of Cricket owes nothing to time, the witch that haunts those drivers in those trucks, that man behind the black windows.

Still, it is the weekend, and far from the Imperium. Here at St. George's the bowler is a skinny East Indian youth, hatless, his white shirt-tail flopping, red hightop running shoes skittering on the perfect green. We are amateurs. It is the weekend. These are the greenswards of Vancouver in the summer.

In the shade of the school building some dowagers in straw hats are clapping their gloved hands for the East Indian lad who has just been bowled out. They clap quite vigorously to show good sportsmanship, and because the centre of the field of play is a hundred meters away, and because there arent many of them there to applaud. The East Indian lad is unbuckling his shinguards, and now he has nothing to do for the rest of the weekend.

10.

In Kitsilano a gull cries . . .

He could go to the beach.
There is no bodysurfing here,
no rubber-capped lifeguards in big plunging rowboats.

This isnt Australia after all;
it's an inland sea this side of the long island that fronts the Japanese
ocean.

The inlet is full of sails among the biding freighters. The blue
mountains rise like a travel brochure. You have all seen the
advertising. The long stretches of sand are covered with red bathing
suits and portable stereos. But sand and french fries in cardboard
boxes are not the park.

And lying down in the sun
is a magazine idea full of fun.

> (I think I hear
> a basketball on cement,
>
> squeaky feet, a bit
> of "Epistrophy") (horn)

But here on the coast of greater Vancouver,
            the parks begin one step from the sand.
At Kits Beach, the strand for the flower people in the Sixties,
            frisbies waft long flights over deep green grass,
and German Shepherds catch them,
            leaping like Houston Rockets
to pull a plastic plate from the sun.

> Where they go to leave their defecation is a mystery.

> (I do hear basketball cement,
> I see)

These well-tanned salt air basketball players never leap that high,
but the stomachs that leap with them are not German Shepherd stomachs.

They say "oof,"
they say "agh, God,"
but there's no referee at the beach.

They are perhaps a reproof to the weekending motorcycle dudes
white as basement potato tendrils, sprawled on the bumpy sand
not even hiding their beer, tattoes announcing clichés
about a world where the sun never shines like this.

Forget about them.

11.

(That's not a saxophone,
that's some corny
thing

Forget about the beach.
This is Victoria Park, a lumpy block of grass
    and pieces of old cigarette package silver in Little Italy.
Men who are probably younger than they look are playing *bocce*.
We are not in Kerrisdale, not at Terminal City.
This is the East End, all right?
Where nobody rolls a flat lawn made rich with horse defecation.

At the west end of the park a sensitive Parks Board has built several
official *bocce campos*. They are twenty-three meters long, 2.4 meters
wide, with a level surface of clay, enclosed with boarded ends and sides
forty-five and thirty centimeters high respectively.

Nobody is using them.

These men are rolling their *bocce* toward the *boccino* at eccentric
angles across the well-worn grass of the park.
It is not quiet as the Kerrisdale Lawn Bowling Club, visitors welcome.
There is a constant mock-emotional jabber of Italian, as the
Commercial Drive heroes cluster round the target and describe fate.

They are wearing no whites at all,
they are wearing Sicilian clothes, brown sweaters and old black suit
trousers in the northern sun.
There are coats hanging in the low branches of linden trees.
Once in a while the little white ball comes to rest
near a clean brown chicken bone.

. . . an accordion)

•

These men, turning their backs on the wooden frames, and striking out
across the uneven green, are proper hearts in the city's parks. They are
the boys of summer.

(Take the most popular team sport in the world—soccer, football,
footie, as they call it back home in Australia, or is that Ozzie Rules.

In the stadia where the World Cup is being played, it is
interesting only in the stands and in the bars later that night. On
the mowed and figured pitch it is an excruciatingly boring game,
made up primarily of delaying tactics and failed strategies.

But on the ground behind a desultory factory in Paraguay, or in
a corner of a sloping park in the east end of Vancouver, Canada,
where they play with bare backs, and cast-off shirts are goal posts,
the game is just what the Creator was thinking of
inventing on the eighth day of Genesis.)

•

So these less-than-paradisaic *bocce* players.
They keep score, presumably, they will have something to boast
at the cappuccino bar late in the afternoon.
They make it worthwhile being a poet with a Saturday off
on the west coast.

And if you have been sitting on a park bench, watching them for a while,
you will have noticed that at a table in the far corner of Victoria Park
there is a cluster of older men in sweaters.
If you amble over and have a look you will see that they are playing cards,
some Mediterranean game that requires two decks and a studied silence.

It could easily have been played in someone's kitchen
or the back room of the *Caffé Volare*. In the winter it is.

•

Harp, harp!

•

But this is summer. We have waited all winter for this.
All winter the equipment has been resting in the trunk of the Toyota.
The regular glove. The first base trapper. The Nike turf shoes.
The baseball cap from Trans Northern Airways. The wrist bands.
The knee braces. The sunburn lotion. The Neet's Foot Oil.
The batting glove. The strap for eyeglasses. The aluminum bat.
The five softballs that rolled in the trunk every turn the Toyota took
in January.

We are the Bad Backs, currently in first place in our league.
We are poets & novelists, painters & reporters, editors & reviewers.
We are getting pretty old.
We are boys & girls.
We have aches & pains.
We have tremendous batting averages.
We dont drink beer before the game.
We have the worst base-runners at Mackenzie Park.

We love Sundays & Thursdays & each other.
We compare bandages.
We play eager softball & call it baseball.
We deride each other's tee shirts.
We pray that no one in our families
                    has a funeral on Sunday or Thursday.

———

—I dont care if I never get back.

———

Since the founding of the famous Cosmic League in May, 1971
we've played ball in over a hundred parks and schoolyards,
on grass on the west side and gravel on the east side,
under the blazing sun and slanting January rain.
Once we pulled off a triple play, and two of us are still alive.
We would rather be in a park on the west coast of Canada
than be locked in the wine cellar of the Chateau Frontenac.

The larks—

We love to play in Douglas Park, green and sloping, long and narrow,
in the very heart of the city.

And we arent the only ones. Ball teams
play there. Jamaican cricket teams play there. Asian soccer teams
play there.

Venerable *Tai Chi* women play with the wind there.

A lone saxophone man plays there.

ten
   or
      more
         off
ten

True lovers of baseball love the saxophone. This young
guy looks like a pretty fair outfielder, but for the past
three summers he has been standing alone in the middle
of Douglas Park, playing old standards on his forlorn
sax. Kids stand around and gawk, their parents twenty
steps behind them. Old folks make requests. If there
were still deer in the parks they would probably come
from Miles around. They say a beautiful woman
followed him out of Ottawa but she looked back and
was lost. If you are in the heart of Vancouver, go to
Douglas Park and listen.

There is probably someone like him in Australia.
Australia is a lot like Vancouver in the summer. They
play rugger there, too.

(With a—
[Bang, crunch, agh, grunt, snarl, thump, rip!]

•

        McBride
        Park
        Oppenheimer
        Park,
        home of the great Japanese baseball teams
        Pandora
        Park

All winter the parks will be green,
                and in the parks
the shades of kids and dads,
              running from base to base,
throwing balls,
       falling over dogs,
           dutifully dropping
ice cream wrappers in trash barrels,
            a lot of
shouting under trees filled with the shades of leaves.

•

(And across the field,
         real estate plotters wondering
who to bribe,
       to grab all that green and call it
undeveloped.)

        Riley
        Park
        Valdez
        Park
        Marpole

Park
lies on top of the great Fraser Midden, the old, old
graveyard of the Musqueam people. Beside the
river their bones lie. Under the running footfalls
of many-coloured children their spirits make
music in the park.

●

Out of the saxophone bell
the small birds fly
to alight like notes
on crooked staves.

———

Paulette Jiles and others

Paulette Jiles In Whitehorse

All over Whitehorse and the
long hills above the Yukon River
there's Paulette Jiles bent a little,
pointing her camera. She knows

what she's looking for. I see
he squinchy face I've grown
to admire, see it gaze in
upon itself, or so I thought, but no,

she's composing whatever wants
to be inside the frame later
that day. She's wearing
the wrong shoes for this crusted snow

but there she goes, and my eyes
like joined lenses go with her,
bent over as she is in her
decorated parka. I seldom

write a poem, but Paulette
told me she doesnt like to see
poets mentioning other poets
in their poems, doesnt like

that kind of frame. I just
had to break my silence,
remembering just now how Paulette
Jiles lookt in front of those

snowy smooth mountains, in the view
finder of her camera I was holding.

Smaro Kamboureli In The Foothills

The bus to the barbecue ranch was held up
by a passel of cowboys with kerchiefs up
to their eyes.

Most of them sat their hosses while one of
them entered the bus, his hogleg drawn, &
moseyed down the aisle, hot basalt in his
eyes.

Smaro leaned forward against her spaghetti
straps: "I'll do anything you want," she de-
clared.

& the desperado's eyes turned into panicked
frogs.

He retreated, his mask fallen around his neck
now, & he turned before he went down the
steps, a three-tooth gap in his lonely bunk-
house grin.

Thea Bowering In Oliver

You stand, laughing, wet-haired,
up to your knees in the lake I crawled through
at your age, laughing at mine.

You are on the other side of the wire fence,
sleek in the water you've stepped from,
the pool in my home town,
where I dawdled afternoons away.

You run from me across the field
where younger than you I ran third
in a three-boy race, faster than I.

Drawing a few days of your childhood
upon by boyhood's landscape,
I make memory not a servant but a poem
through which you scamper, a brownish
butterfly in the sun. A daughter,
a metaphor, a sister to my first years.

Nicole Brossard In The Badlands

Everyone else stood on the edge. While she
didnt even think of it. Quebeckers

meet their own deadlines. [

                                                    ]

Later in the new building filled with bones
balanced on each other, she wondered whether

she should do the difficult. [
     ] Please do, we said, please do read.

Pauline Butling In Campbell Lake

The water of Campbell Lake is very cold,
& Pauline Butling is in it.

Her limbs are long & white, the glacier
is white, her one-piece bathing suit

is pale. She is still here
thirty years after our adult lives began,

doing the breast stroke in Campbell
Lake.

I have never been in love with her
but I would kill anyone

who tried to drown her. I would like
the sun to take the time to tan her,

to warm the water a little.

YARDS

Mexico City 1964

Sergio Mondragón was a Yoga teacher
and a vegetarian, so he was nervous
when I went under the grandstand for tacos.

These were closed-up tacos,
deep-fried in corn oil, and there were only
two kinds of tacos.

                         The outfielders
stood on the warning track—at 7,700 feet
fly balls carry. Pitchers aim at heads.

There were cheese tacos and brain tacos,
queso or *seso*. Both fillings were white.
Sergio was not confident of my Spanish.

Suitcase Simpson played left field for Mexico City.
A Cuban kid named Peña pitched for Puebla.
Sergio poked his taco open with his thumb
and sniffed it.

This was one of the happiest August days in my life.
I had never seen a big league ball game.
No one fired a *pistola* in the bleachers.

I was an inveterate Mexcity fan.
I once accused the umpire of *blasfemia*.
I was proud of bringing Sergio a *taco de queso*.

Nürnberg Stadion 1966

A tiny sign shaped like an arrow
pointed to the right, just said "Stad."

But remember "Triumph of the Will"?
—thousands of jubilant Nazis, eerie Romans
in black and white, like fangs on a jumping dog.

Now a paved road goes through the wall,
a dozen concrete-mixer trucks are lined up
before *der Führer's* reviewing stand, the marble eagles
are long removed. We see high epic steps

and a foreman calmly gesturing,
his arm held forward and up, my skin
did not crawl, but just the same—
he was showing a truck driver where to park.

Tony and I climbed, as nineteen years later
I would wander Berlin's 1936 Olympic stadium,
to be where history was. It seems, really,
ephemeral. We see sun-bleached stone and
the grass needs mowing.

                    But the size. Riefenstahl's camera
could not deliver the size. We stood and looked out
over acres of grass inside the walls.
                    At the far end
there was an American football field in one corner,
and in the other corner a baseball park.

Tiger Stadium 1967

For twenty-two years Greg Curnoe
has been apologizing because we didnt stay
for the second game.
                    Okay, how about one
and a half innings, I said, and so we went.

Briggs Stadium when I was a kid, now
the first big league game I ever see,
my stupidly dear Red Sox, their pennant year at last,
here to visit the Tigers. We sat in right, second deck,

where Dick McAuliffe, .239, parked one. It's
the ball green created to look like
the typical beautiful 1945 big league park.

The outfield grass is mowed like a chess board.
The overhanging roof was on News Of The World,
Oliver Theatre Saturday Matinee. The Tigers'
bright white home uniform the classiest in baseball.

Carl Yastrzemski, .326, was there, I don't remember what he did.
I dont remember the score of the first game.
I remember the tidy bleachers in center, closed off
for the hitters' background.

It was Centennial Year across the river in Canada,
but Briggs Stadium is history right now for me.
Greg Curnoe is a perverse lacrosse student,
collects magazines about European cycling,
thinks George Chuvalo is a great Canadian.

I graciously wave off his apology every time,
and remember he never showed me
the Intercounty League stadium in London, Ont.

Parc Jarry 1969

There are thirty thousand aluminum
seats at Jarry Park, and on Bat Day
fifteen thousand kids are banging
free miniature Louisville Sluggers on them.

A not quite major league noise, but
if you enjoy clang and if you can tolerate
a guy playing a violin on the Expos' dugout roof
you'll put up with it.

To be almost major league,
to watch Bob Gibson walk in
from the dressing room at the right field foul pole.

There's no grandstand, just metal bleachers all around,
and a guy in a toque
who buys a seat beside him behind third
for his duck, a leash on its neck.

Even in the out of town papers
there's Montreal listed in the National League standings,
and my New Yorkish Cornell Berkeley buddy Ed Pechter
eats five hotdogs, no mustard, no relish.

But jeepers, Jarry Park. They play softball
just outside left field, kids kick their feet
in the pool just past right. This is
a community park, what's Cincinnati doing here?

Fenway Park 1971

A perfect location, behind and beside
the Yankee dugout, these lovely box seats
are surprisingly cheap, the green wall in left
is painted concrete, a baffle this side of the highway.

Here the game isnt over till the last ball's out.

My friend Ed Pechter is a Yankees fan
with a New Yorkish childhood. He knows
enough about beisbol to know I'm a serious
Boston devotee, martyr, sacrifice, supplicant
yearning for more of this goddamn real life.

The PA voice I've heard for years on TV
is loud over mid-city air, Back Bay accent
turning names into peanut brittle.

This is a typical Fenway game, bang,
Ed's up waving his short arms, hotdog, counter-bang,
I'm up with 30,000 college students
and morning cab drivers. Bang, up goes Ed

for the last time, then Petrocelli
turns his bat in a tight little arc, and we win
8-4, the ball a bright moon over the far road.

Back in the cafeteria the waitress says
"Black or reguhluh?" I say reguhluh
and I've been having it that way ever since.

The Kingdome 1974

We got seats high behind home plate,
Dwight and Paul and I, looked down
at a big green pinball machine!

The ball should boing off the shortstop,
Boeing! 50,000 points, five free games.
Here in the Great North West, rain

outside the grey concrete roof, sea full of perch
beyond the Ocean Isles in the fog, Mariners
an expansion ball team forever.

Dwight catches a foul ball
but he has to drop his beer to get it.
What is the American League doing in the rain forest?

Is coming to Seattle really coming to the U.S.A.?
Old coots with caulked boots crack peanuts and jokes,
nice working class slim fellows in the bleachers;

they're kind of Canadians, kind of too hip
to be Canadians, baseball's been in the North West
as long as the railroad.

But they used to play between rainfalls; now
it's pinball, colours flashing, now Dwight and Paul
and I stomp our feet hard for a rally against the Yanks

and the whole place shuts down dark
except for the simple scoreboard lights
that spell TILT, game over, good night.

Olympic Stadium 1977

Dwight Gardiner led me out of the Metro,
across some concrete and through a door

into a loud burst of light, huge circle
of yellow, red, blue, and special green!

Still batting practice, I saw a bat flash
and then crack, crack, crack, cra-hack

echoed round the abandoned legend, a ghost
of the games. We settled in. Four attendants

sold us a beer. I saw eight people in uniforms
dusting off seats in one empty section.

This is labour in Quebec. Eventually
somebody came to bat, probably San Diego,

my kind of luck. Yes, I said to Dwight, he's
back this week from Bolivia, it is *très grand*

but everything is so far away—the infield,
the National League pennant, America.

High above, the disc of grey-blue sky
is empty. At least at little Parc Jarry

we could watch the new Boeing 747s
hang in the low sky. If the score was

St. Louis 10, Expos 0, we could
look over the right field fence, check out

the swimmers in the pool, the kite fliers
with their daddies Sunday afternoon.

Big Boy Stadium 1978

Puerto Limón, Costa Rica is a Graham Greene town
except for Big Boy Stadium,
                                    square concrete,
clumps of dusty weeds, lorn wooden benches
with maybe four old coots sitting
                                    apart from each other,
Black guys with all their shirt buttons done up.

Dwight told me about this park
and Billy Boy Hamburgers in San José,
the national cuisine.

                    It's February tenth,
on the tenth parallel, sun directly over
the sunburnt part in my hair, but here in the cool
shade I watch a familiar sinewy old coach
loft high expert fungos to three eager young men,
their waists as narrow as a breath of mary smoke.

They dont do everything right, they are grandsons
of Jamaican banana slaves, weird English voices
in Spanish Central America, old fashioned crack of the bat
and I sit in my dark rest, get under the ball
and throw it right, one hop to the plate.

No one turns to look. Now the three are in closer,
pretending to be infielders, bending.

                            When does the season start?
The old coach is black like my white granddad,
the three shortstops a few years away
from a decent double play.

Hi Corbett Field 1982

There were fourteen drops of rain in Phoenix
and all the Cactus League games were cancelled,
so I drove to Tucson, along one of my favourite roads
in a rough red Datsun.

The Indians versus the A's, seven thousand old geeks
and this travelling Canadian poet at Corbett,
where the P.A. is shouted down every few minutes
by huge black fighter planes from SAC.

What a nice little park, like Bailey in Vancouver
without the gentle hill of cedar trees;
but here the March 16 sun beats on my head,
my arms will be burnt, the part in my hair red.

Billy Martin wears a spring smile instead of Gotham sneer,
a Durante nose, a cross made of straight pins
on the front of his cap. Thank the Lord.
He's going to win this in the ninth.

Bowie Kuhn is introduced between jets.
He stands in the box seat behind home,
waves his big new straw hat. All the geezers
say "Boo" good and loud. He smiles:
maybe they're saying "Bowie."

But most important of all—it worked.
You can get to the park, stand in a line,
get a seat with all the old birds in holiday clothes,
and watch a big league ball game
                       in the hot sun
in March, in Tucson.
                 One of the two nicest
cities in the American west.

Aloha Stadium 1983

In the grandstand the old Japanese men
consume miso soup and noodles
　　　　out of styrofoam packages.

The Islanders are on a road trip in Oregon
but the Rainbow Warriors are home to Arizona State.

The center field bleachers move,
　　　　they are on wheels. When baseball
replaces football they roll half the stands
　　　　over the artificial turf, green Oahu.

　　　　　　　　This
is Pearl Harbor. What a gyp, I said out loud,
USS Arizona is under water.

　　　　　　　The college kids
use aluminum bats; that echoing ping
seems right if you're a mainland stranger,
that deep green plastic on an island covered with paradise foliage.

You're trying to swallow Mickey Big Mouth Beer
and thinking *Tora Tora Tora*,
but all you hear is ping ping ping.

The old Japanese men never clap their bony hands,
　　　　never shout hooray, manipulate *ohashi*,
remember Babe Luth, forget the navy under the sea;

we're all halfway between Tokyo and San Diego,
　　　　in the bottom of the sixth,
looking at the seam running across right field.

Oppenheimer Park 1984

In Japantown, a hill to climb in right field,
deep deep death valley in left; funny name

for a Tokyo park. Here, 1930, Powell Street Grounds,
great Japanese ball teams got famous across Canada;

hard to imagine them now, earnest and skinny
Nipponese baseball heroes, athletes and fishermen

stretching a double, sliding on hard dirt,
frowning in late sunshine between flat roofs.

Now here we are, ex-Kozmik League ruffians,
putting on the best show we can, derelict jockoes,

we love history even when we dont know it,
we hit foul balls into traffic of Powell Street,

try to hold our opposition to fifteen runs,
swing three slender tin bats in the on deck circle.

Some circle! Guy leans against the wire fence
talking to a pink drunk with paper sack.

The audience numbers between ten and nineteen all day,
some asleep in the sun, some sarcastic,

some Indian outfielders from the north coast.
No one would rather play anywhere else than here.

If you foul out here you'll get a laugh.
If you play your cards right you'll get home free.

But you'll have to pick your way among ghosts;
some of them wear bandannas under their caps.

A Stroke Of Luck 1985

I rode in a taxi cab to the airport at Perth
in Western Australia with Doris Lessing, what fortune!

She looked exactly like her photographs, braids
exactly right. I love gum trees, she said,

they remind me of my childhood in that other heat,
I'm heading south along the coast to see more. Now

I love gum trees too, but just along here
I expect, there it is, the sign says baseball.

They're playing the 1985 Australian championship,
whoops, out of sight, no day games in this heat anyway.

Ah, Ms Lessing, in 1988 I took a cab alone and we drove
toward the airport. There'll be a baseball park

right here, there it is, I said. The taxi driver
shook her head. I wouldnt know, I'm an old Scot, she said.

Roma 1985

Annalise Goldoni was driving us back from Villa Lante,
through light wet snow, through March rain,

while I wondered, how do you read the middle class
in a country marked by old broken walls?

Automotive wheels where Etruscans walked,
a roof to the left fallen in during World War II.

I suppose I was reminded of windows
on moving *paesaggio*, next to the Indian Ocean.

I said while writing one of my novels
I looked out the train window, north of Bologna, saw

three boys playing December baseball on an open green,
running above bones of Roman field hands.

I have never seen baseball in Italy, she said.
But just then I looked down to my right:

at the foot of the gentle hill there appeared a
baseball diamond, backstop, wooden stands, empty.

Gone in a flash of trees. I faced forward.
That garden at Villa Lante, I said,

it must be better looking
in the summer sunshine, say mid-season.

Anaheim Stadium 1986

I should have known.
Five years ago I got off a Pan Am 747 at LAX
with four hundred and thirty South Americans.

We stood in two long lines at immigration
to show our pasaportes to a white woman
or a black man with aviator glasses.

Neither of them spoke any Spanish
in El Pueblo de la Reyna de los Angeles.

Now Thea and I are in the left field stands
at Anaheim Stadium, Orange County, filled with old folks
sitting beside portable radios.

It's a beautiful summertime gloaming dusk stadium
with that high haloed Alpha dead centre field.

Stands for Alimentación, I told myself,
sent the kid for nachos, looked at the Jays
scoring two runs.

She comes back, *¡que lástima!*
It's the same melted cheez-whiz on chips
you get in Vancouver and Edmonton,

but the little fourteen-year-old dearie
knows what's what, she saved the day
with a half-pound of free *jalapeños*
scattered on the fake orange goo.

Now that's hot, I said,
and so were the Jays, winning 2-0.

Exhibition Stadium 1986

Going to the game with David McFadden
you really need three seats,
such as here above the flat fog,
last game of the season, KC in town.

He has a thick jacket and a big shoulder bag.
We climb steep stairs to the top,
huge hoagies in our hands, I cant escape
the alliteration, that's how to fix this,
and really big waxy cups of Pepsi or something.

He settles like a hen on a dozen eggs,
puts down Pepsi and one-bite-gone hoagie;
out comes portable radio with ear plugs (good citizen),
out comes home-made scorebook, printed on computer.

Out come field glasses to catch signs
off runner at second getting them off catcher,
who gets them with turn of head out of dugout;
out comes Toronto Maple Leafs baseball cap.

Out comes Captain Midnight decoder fountain pen,
out comes one-dollar cigar, out comes Blue Jay yearbook,
McFadden takes a bite out of hoagie,
out comes sauerkraut all over fan in second-last row.

All right, the fog clears for a while, gulls descend,
Jesse Barfield hits home run number forty
and strikes out every other appearance. Every time
Lloyd Moseby comes up I yell
"Come on, Quaker!" McFadden says "Shaker!"

Then Dave lifts the plug out of one ear.
"He's hitting .271," he says. I remember
this is the lad who started a poetry magazine
in Hamilton, Ontario, imagine that!

Nat Bailey Stadium 1987

Sitting in famous Section 9 with our friends,
we see a wide purple sunset,
silhouette hillside with besom cedar trees,
a first place team gettin by on pitching.

Triple A uniforms can be a little embarrassing,
word too long on the hat, too much yellow and red on the visitors;
there are only three umpires, sometimes two,
the organist doesnt know his job, plays older goldies.

"The prettiest park in professional baseball."
"The most beautiful city in the world."
Some idiots in Section 8 bring their cellular phones.
Yes, we're more world-class than world-class Toronto.

But come on, you're with Fast Eddie & Paulie,
it's the sixth inning, a little dew in the night air—
where would you rather be? Some cathedral in Seville?
You want them to move the Canadians and the Phoenix Firebirds
under the dome downtown?

Never win a year's supply of Pepsi-Cola,
never attend when the Famous Chicken is in town,
sit down resolutely when some drunk boys try to start a wave,
applaud the number eight batter who hits a grounder behind the runner.

And when you go home, if you have to go home,
maybe there will be highlights on the TV news.

Municipal Stadium 1988

It should have been my father that was here,
he a Cleveland Indians fan for no known reason,
no geography—
                        only major league game he saw
was in Montreal, 1970.

                        Here the Mistake by the Lake,
nearly empty, or seven thousand good-natured souls
against the ever-present Kansas City Royals.

To show my skill I boo Bill Buckner, .241,
for insisting on wearing a glove in the '86 Series.

My companions were born to this;
I had to earn it, a boy in Okanagan sand,
now sitting in baseball's biggest park,

old as the century, old as the league, old
as Hart Crane, throw me a lifesaver.

My companions and I had ethnic sandwiches
in a real U.S. bar, sports photos on the wall.

They respect me, they want to know
what I can tell them. I sit in that old yard

and celebrate. I made it here. I think of my Dad,
and act unlike him, exactly,
loud mouth, cheering the Tribe,
sardonic, in love, broken in the ball park.

HHH Metrodome 1989

This is Minnesota, every blue plastic seat
has a blue plastic ring to hold
the beer container for the person behind.
The beer is made in Wisconsin, it's pasteurized.

This canvas-top billowing baseball tent show
is clean as downtown Portland, Oregon.
Everyone in section 126 has blond hair.
Hubert Humphrey is buried behind second base.

Every pinstriper out there on the green plastic
has the word TWINS on his chest,
though there is only one man per uniform.

I'm with Dennis Cooley, who knows something about baseball
though he's from Saskatchewan, and David Arnason,
who knows something. I'm making a fool of myself
as always, loud and touched by mortality.

I love this, the upper middle west, the Norwegian
big leagues, Kirby Puckett's ass
is even bigger than it looks on television.

Everyone in section 126 has a clean face,
the prairie sun fights its way through the roof,
we are Canadians cheering for Blue Jays,
who are losing badly—
                    this is perfect.

This is the way to make your hosts comfortable,
pleasing you and beating your Birds, buying you
another American beer one afternoon in the Hump.

New Year's Day 1990

Past two blonde heads,
from the little window of a very old Boeing,
I saw Shea Stadium standing lonely in the wet
beyond the airport fence.

The Mets were supposed to represent the National League
in 1989.

Bouncing down over Lake Ontario
under the fish-grey clouds and the brown clouds,
the plane tilted its window so I saw
a tall tower and the so-called Sky Dome.

The Blue Jays were called to represent the American League
in 1989.

That was some World Series we missed,
some auspicious morning
for the Gay Nineties.

Candlestick Park 1990

Medium jacket on, I was the only passenger
on the long turn turn bus ride to the Stick,

walked alone as nearly always
to the ticket seller in the heated booth.

Suffered a quick frisk by a Black woman in black uniform—
was she searching for a gun or a can of outlaw beer?

Eight months after the World Series earthquake
I walked up the ramp with confidence, medium jacket

but I saw dozens I mean dozens of pistol and long club police
& a few mouse-faced tattoo freaks with blankets.

The Stick got colder & colder, the Chicago Cubs
hit home runs from time to time, people around me up high

could have been out on recreation passes, I looked for handcuffs,
everyone got drunker & nastier. I came to San Francisco

with a flower in my hair, and I left town
with my hand over my empty wallet. At the Stick

I said this is the smallest hotdog I've ever seen,
& the guy in front of me said have a look at this little beer.

On the way back into town I stood up all the way,
mean exterior walls bouncing by, my left hand over my heart.

Oliver Community Park 1948

Familiar sun
declined is hasting now with prone career
to the Ocean Isles, and rising are some few bedraggled stars,

not to mention what I recall of my home town
ball field, 1990, weather-grey wooden grandstand
that would crash like a giant accordion
if four strong infielders full of beer
lined up and gave it a good shove.

We took oranges to the ball field, later
used the skins to cup water from the tap.

Willy and I wandered the perimeter trying to sell
Orange Crush and peanuts in the shell.
Other Sundays we pursued foul balls
through the deep rattlesnake grass for Elks Club dimes.

Once, age fifteen, I hit a single
with the bases loaded, but went next week
for work out of town,
                          where I still am,
and that was my real career.

They dont play ball there now, television
and then golf courses arrived,
highways became easy to use, money dropped by.

The tall wooden grandstand with the roof
stood through four decades of winters,
forty years of family picnics elsewhere,
power boats on small green lakes.

                          I went to
Quebec, I forgot the P.A. announcer's voice echoing
off the center-field scoreboard.

MARILYN

Joe & Marilyn

His loneliness that came out between his teeth like a smile
she recognized, and she should have been frightened
as she was when she saw low-flying geese like an arrow of eiderdown
flying straight west.

                But she was not, this he saw
as she put on her oversized gentleman glasses and took the wheel,
driving the Italian car fast thru the narrow streets
of a city he only now cared to know by night.

At the Indian restaurant he tumbled into love
before she had cut the steam from her pastry.
The windows behind her might as well have been paintings,
his smile gone and his bottom lip threatening to go with it.

In yesterday's real life he was an assured success
with good hands and a quick release. She looked directly
across at him and he felt her long bony hands
deep inside, among the disordered remains of his viscera.

Arthur & Marilyn

There was a bar in the afternoon with some kind of athletes'
photographs in frames on the wall, and he was in it.

But he was not looking at sport, he was looking at a woman
with give me something eyes, a woman unlike any
he had ever seen while he was awake, but wished he had.

Not that she was perfect, that would have been dreadful;
rather he had apparently downed several glasses of beer
or something as benign, and didn't feel his stomach.

She was not an extension of his fancy; when she smiled
at last all legitimacy in Freud rolled over the footboard
of the back door like a dented empty barrel.

Her bare arms shone in the window, a kind of prose
he wanted to write as fast as he could when he woke up.

She was talking and talking in a language he knew,
and he would never tell anyone what she said;
he would only save any moment he could, and publish it in hell.

John & Marilyn

Now he knows
what it means, sick
with love, sick—

know? Yes,
it is more like know than feel,
it is knowing
there is a she not here
here. There is she
he thinks of always
as you.

That is because he speaks
all day to her,
that absent
lack of his health.

He's long time wondered
whether he'd ever
write love poems addressed
to a you. You know
it all, you
missing nurse.

Robert & Marilyn: A Valediction Forbidding Morning

Our two souls, hello to them again,
good night sweet lobby
of this undistinguished hotel.

Yes, there are harms, there are
fears out there, and up there,
I mean on the road,
where we are going;

shut the curtain, close away
the parking lot, the moon behind it,
open my heart again
in our barely practised way.

I've told you of your left eye,
how sad it is, how
it is my favourite. Open that eye

and look into this heart,
it loves to see you here at last;
it knows it could be left
on an oily debris highway

while red and blue
roof lights turn, while
they pick up everything.

The Great Grandchildren Of Bill Bissett's Mice

A bright metal called trumpet, called
Chet Baker, maybe
a dozen hard notes, reaches
right now

to a working waterfront. Gulls, tugs, foghorn, could be
winches and davits, quiet spill to wave-slap against
pilings at last.

In the late Eighties the water round the necessary
city of Vancouver is for fun, for boats and play. It is
another place to show off your designer sunglasses.

Uh huh.

But in the late Fifties the waterfront was for ships
and high piles of lumber, for men in dark knitted caps
working on vessels with red stars on their funnels.
Vancouver was a sea port. All through downtown a
young newcomer could smell the salt. That's gone.
Downtown is bank towers. Downtown is Toronto.

The trumpet was likely Chet Baker.
Had to keep polishing the luster,
keep the salt out of it.

1958. I was all alone. I wanted to walk solitary
down by the waterfront, in black and white, mostly
black. I was gathering material, drowning myself in
atmosphere. The lonely American novelist.

I came down from the dry brown Okanagan Valley,
and came all the way down to the water. To be a
writer who mattered. The Okanagan Valley looked

like a western movie. This wet dark Vancouver looked
like the latest thing. It was mysterious and open, this
waterfront. It was not far from Hamburg and Burma.
It was instructive.

(It was romantic.)

It was romantic. I was alone, sitting in waterfront
beer parlours, a book open on the torn and wet terry
cloth. But I was listening, the solitary writer.

Art Pepper. You have to imagine, remember,
get out your old thirty-three
and a thirds.

He didnt cover anyone
but the waterfront.
If you like.

> Hear? Your friends were listening to Gene Vincent
> but the solitary writer in the old blue air force
> trench coat was listening to the suicidal jazz guys.

> Zwah badaza zwah da da—

> I did not tap my foot or snap my fingers. I was
> cool. I had a set of drum brushes, and I could shhhhh,
> I could hear. All the young Vancouver writers
> came from the musical hills. Lionel Kearns and Fred
> Wah came down to Vancouver from the West
> Kootenays, to write poems. Lionel brought his
> saxophone. Fred brought his trumpet.

(I brought mine.)

> Gladys Hindmarch came over from Vancouver Island
> with her alto. Frank Davey left his piano at home in
> Abbotsford, but he and Bobby Hogg showed up in their
> coupés, ready to go.

> Daphne Marlatt was here as a girl. She saw them coming:

They came from small towns and no towns in the in-
terior from the north and the island.

They came with their solitary dreams, looking for a
page to write something entirely new on.

But I came from the British Empire. I was a girl in
Conrad country. I was born into colonial British, a
language my mother gave me and tried to keep
herself, here, next to the deep trees, the dark
between the trees and in the hearts of these people.

I grew up wanting to learn the language of this place.

> I thought she did all right. She did say things very
> carefully, like one of those touching girls with
> hopeless hair in British black and white movies. Her
> small mouth closed carefully over the word "no."

> But she dug into the watershed and learned the language,
> and learned that there were numerous languages.

> She said:

> > *small*
>
> *single flower*

> > *by the sea (Salt does, Asphalt*
> *cuts thru time, your eye, my tongue, down where a*
> *culvert mouths on the beach the city's underground:*
> *You come thru walking, corpses, bits of metal,*
> *bird cry.*

Downtown, then, from the dock
sound
carried,
salt drifted through the air, we
were always there.

People from the middle of the United States called Vancouver the most beautiful city in the world, and public relations writers here did too.

But the isolate and lordly novelist down from the bush knew it was ugly, too. There were telephone pole back alleys crooked and glinting hard under the greasy sun. Old toothless men lying on the street in purple eighty-nine cent sleep got sharp boot toes in the ribs and head, and the young writer in the old blue rain coat walked on by, practising how to dangle a cigarette from his bottom lip.

Lots of police
sirens on Hastings Street, gone to get
someone who's
no relation.

There were isolate country writers all over town. Somehow our individual hungers got us to the same places, and we learned another way of being young hotshots. We learned to be a group. We learned how to be dangerous. Gentle and dangerous, and smoking cigarettes.

We decided to write a city and call it Vancouver.

(What about Kits.?
What about Yew Street?)

All the streets named after trees would plunge steep into Kitsilano's tidy bay. Pine Street. Chestnut. Maple. Yew trees are for poets in graveyards; we all know that. All these tree streets are lined with expensive condos now. Two decades ago they offered cheap housing and warehousing for students and out of work marijuana boys and girls. How ignorant Vancouver was, how innocent.

Nowadays how can you avoid a voice, says
You got water. You got mountain views. You got
valuable real estate.

Yew Street was full of poets and artists. When I close
my eyes and see that hill and those people on the
slant sidewalk, I fall in love with them all. Right now.
I am the ghost they might have felt whispering by
them a morning glory day in 1963.

Or hiking the steep concrete below their windows at night.

A manual typewriter at some distance, and a little
ambient street noise, a car honk in the distance, a
1962 radio song. Typewriter and trumpet—who's leaving?

Did you ever hear such a thing? All along the summer street
the typewriters at the open windows. Where are all those
novels now, those poems and those novels?

Driftwood
            piles up on the beach
people
            pile up on the beach
buildings
            torn down and reborn
year after year
within sight of the sea.

No room for ghost towns
out here on the edge of things;
no place for ghosts.

That's the end of a poem from that night. It was

written by my friend Frank Davey. He and I are both
ghosts now, walking with soft quiet feet through
those rightful immigrant poems about our city.
He is a charter member of my gang called by all kinds
of names, some unkind, some accurate, called Tish,
called West Coast. I always argued with him and then
told his detractors to take the long view, wait and see.

How could a young poet have detractors? But that's
the sort of thing that happened. Bill Bissett fell on his
head. Red Lane's head let him down and he died.
Jamie Reid's head lead him away to some pretty
streets and then some ugly avenues, and then most
of the way home.

I argued with all of them. I never dismissed any of
them. I argued in public with Lionel Kearns. Then I
went looking for him. Here is what I said about that.
You will notice that I did not do what they told me to
do in creative writing school at UBC: I didnt find my
own voice.

I look for him under a disorderly pile of papers where
he is looking for something. The print comes off in my
hands and floats around the room. The letter double
you folds as it falls, it flutters. He watches it ab-
sorbed as if that was what he was looking for.

I look for him under a disorderly pile of letters where
he is looking for something written by somebody and
he needs it right now, the telephone is nowhere in
sight, it must be under a pile of numbers offering
information we cant do without. He says it is right
here somewhere probably under a book of concrete
poems by a Pakistani in a dry city.

(Right about here I would play a little bit of Zoot Sims.
See whether you can find some.

Ah ah, hmmm hmm—)

I look for him in the phone book and he is everywhere
defending the land and looking for something, either
absorbing change or the danger of change that is
more of the same from somewhere else. The earth
folds on us speck by speck and once in a while a
seed. He laughs and laughs and his mouth is wide
open in the middle of a dusty beard above which are
faded eyes in unprotected pale skin.

I feel like a ghost floating through this poem. I feel
like a run of saxohorn notes.

I look for him in Vancouver 1962 but it is certainly
later than that and we have lines in our pages. His
house used to smell like curry and then it smelled
like soy sauce and now it smells like whole wheat
flour. His old grey socks are under a pile of papers on
which poems have somehow settled and he puzzles
over them, looking for something he knows he has
there somewhere.

Hard shoes walking on a street at night.
Metal on a wet, black brow. Could be John Coal
Train.

John Newlove is our national poet. He has lived
everywhere in Canada. That year he lived on Yew
Street, up some stairs, down the back.

Where you might hear those footsteps. Door creaking open. Hear
Howlin'
Wolf singing one of his slower pieces,
sing "Killing Floor."

hear a frying pan sizzle.

We are just two blocks from Kitsilano Beach in the
moon glint. Newlove is frying up a mess of little

silvery fish. Night time smelt fishers from immigrant families net them at Kitsilano Beach.

They sizzle.

He is a man of extremes in his life. He lives on nothing on the edge of a forest, or he sits in a big city office in a tailored suit. But from the beginning his poems have been one eyeblink this side of perfect.

He is fat and he is thin and parts fall out and it is noted, it is a surprise to note without having thought of it till: now he has no home life save in the poems, through the black prism of the poems.

> The radio plays on and on, variations
> of the same song. The fish crackles as it cooks,
> the mice are quiet. Salt is in the shaker,
> ready to be sprinkled on the eyeless dinner fish.

Two blocks from the beach. At night I went down to get sand for the kitten to pee in. I always looked out under the icy light to see a whale's white belly just once. Just once I wanted to see a wild whale turning over in the night spray, moon slither along its keel. I never did, except in the literature we all made. The mice are quiet.

Seeds rattle quietly.
Rattle and rattle, take on
a shhhh
beat.

> Bill Bissett lived and painted and ran a mimeograph machine downstairs in a kind of big shed next door to Newlove's, a block down the hill from our place. At

our place there was a poet from Toronto and Majorca
upstairs, tearing up the floorboards to hide plants
from Mexico.

Bill Bissett had a baby and a kind of orchestra, or was
that Al Neil? The drummer played the bedsprings. Bill
Bissett was not a phonetic poet. He just broke the
rules, okay? He lived through it. But the mice did too.

A bulldozer ripped his house down.

In the seventies we moved back from Montreal, into
a commune right around the corner. One morning we
woke up to hear and went to the window to see: a
driver under a metal roof butted Bill's old place down
in less than an hour.

The quiet mice had to find a new place to live. We
did not welcome them to our community but they
moved in just the same—the great great
grandchildren of Bill's mice. We were the only house-
hold on York Street without a white cat. All the other
houses had white cats with different-coloured eyes.

I wrote a poem for Bissett, hoping I could perform it
in such a way that the mice would continue west-
ward, to the salt. It went like this:

Round and round he goes and where he stops.

*Round and round he goes and where he stops
Round he goes and where will you find him, no
one seems to find him, round he goes and the
reading stops and he is gone before you have
begun to know, it stops and where is he, you
look round and round but he is gone and then
you stop, he is gone.*

*Round and round he goes and round where he stops
the inky smudge of words of words yes of*

words, oh of words, oh smudge of words, a
smudge of words, round they go, in, and in,
you feel them inside each other, all inside,
round they go, till the letter, I'm thinking
of P, capital P, inside the P is a

Round he goes and knowbody knows. He sent me an
ap parition
er ap
parishioner, round to see me, a wrap
or issue, it was a
blew ointment for my rapt
derision, many years ago, round a
nineteen sixty too, where he stops, an
apt emission, to see, like it was a ghost of
smudgy ink, an inkster, and poet going round & round
inspiration, and instinctual apparition, this whole
thing goes round and round and isnt it ap parent and
isnt it a mazing that round it goes and right here
it stops.

Unquote.
You never give me your whatsiz.
You only give me your da da da da.

> In 1962 we never had enough money but we had this
> huge reservoir of time and this gigantic mountain of
> ideas.
>> The poetry would never run out. We shared the funny
>> paper. Later, later,
>> we would break down.

Footsteps on a wet, black
street, where the elite
never meet.

> Here is the studio of the painter Mike Rice. That is
> what he is called in my stories and novels. His name

in his own life is Gordon Payne. He seems quite
ordinary but he is strange. Early in the morning,
before the seagulls are awake, he is running a few
miles along the beach. In 1962 hardly anyone is
running or jogging or power-walking or eating sen-
sible proteins. On the way back from the run he
walks, picking up dry driftwood for his big brown
barrel stove.

Can you hear "The Rite of Spring" through the wall?

On the big brown stove Mike Rice boils water for tea.
Then he starts drinking tea and painting. He drops the
needle on a black circle of Stravinsky, puts paint-
brushes between every pair of fingers, and leaps at
a wide wide canvas tilted against the wall—

The door is opened
and the "Rite of Spring" is very very loud.

Can you turn that down?

Can you hear me?

Let's go.

Terrific music. Used to listen to that stuff all the
time. But then you get older and mellower. Then if
you are an artist you contemplate. You dont leap
at the canvas any more. Now you ARE the canvas.

Still, I like that Chet Baker, like
night-time footsteps, and whistling.
say whistling
                whatever Chet Baker tune
you were playing at the top.

This is Allen's Alley, if you remember that. Or the
walk made by the Great Guildersleeve. An Allen's
Alley full of 1962 artists.

Young Claude Breeze has a storefront studio just a
block up Yew Street. A sweet squirrel of a new
woman named Judith Copithorne has another store-
front farther up. Gerry Gilbert just went by on his
black bicycle—you cant see him in the dark. If he
is going downhill he doesnt have any brakes. You can
hold your breath and listen for a faint splash. It is a
poem.

Isnt it funny? Years ago on Sherbrooke Street I said:

. . . his great brittle nose rises like roots
from the moist soil of the west coast, his
bicycle lies in parts rusting in some unknown
person's shed.
He carries snails and slugs with him, they are
dry in a match box or moist on a stick from
the soil of his back yard on the coast.
That is what you do down Yew Street on a
bicycle, it is so steep, and it is not funny if
you cannot stop at the bottom.
The better work men do is always under stress
and at great personal loss.
His flesh falls away exposing the bones and
that is exactly what he is coming to let
his poetry do and I come to hear it.

(Damn poets. Thought they owned Kitsilano just be-
cause they lived there in my old apartment rooms;
we had oil drums in the back lane, and that's where
they pumped their fuel to keep the kitchen warm in
the winter.)

That kitchen. We had to sit with our feet in the oven.

(Some of them sold poems from time to time, and
then they went up to Fourth Avenue, to Jackson's
Meats, where you could buy cheddar cheese by the
cent. Seventeen cents worth of cheese. Poets and
painters. Deadbeats.)

> After we all left, the LSD crowd came in. There were
> rainbows in all the windows.

> Nepalese temple bells were breaking up that old
> gang of mine. The hookahs in the head shops had no
> time for the poetry revolution.

(It took a while, but we eventually got the hippies out
and the city hall to listen, And now we have condo-
millions all up the streets from Kitsilano Beach.)

> I drove through there today. I saw the ghost of Sam
> Perry on Cypress Street, holding an old sixteen
> millimetre camera to its eye. I saw the ghost of
> Red Lane ducking into the alley behind First Avenue
> with a brown paper bottle in its transparent hand.

(Dont use your dead artists for your composition.)

> Tell *them* that.

I'd insinuate some quiet Chet Baker music
somewhere around here, enough to shut the dead poets up
eventually.

> (I havent forgotten that at the beginning of this
> memoir you called yourself The Lonely American Novelist,)

> That's all there *was* in 1958.

Hmm, ah!

> First we all met one another and we were not lonely
> any more.

(Ha!)

    We were not lonely writers any more. Then after a
    while we were Canadian novelists and Canadian poets.

(You were going to be Canadian literature.)

    We were Vancouver writing. That is what we still are.
    There are still writers and their machines behind
    those windows, but those windows are now in
    Little Italy, not Kitsilano.

(Not Maclean's Magazine.)

    Not to worry.
    Ha.

    Come for a walk with me.

Listen. You might hear
a wave slap wet pillar.

        It is not as easy as it was thirty years ago, but you
        can still get to the waterfront. If you can get into it
        you can still wear your old blue rain coat. There are
        triangular sails in Burrard Inlet now. The Pacific Rim
        hotels look over everyone's shoulders. Big city. Isnt
        this just what you wanted? It looks a lot better in
        the dark rain. You can smell the sea when you're
        this close now, but it doesnt smell like the sea.

            You have a choice. Step into the oil rainbow water
            and look ridiculous. Or turn around and walk up the
            slope. Get into the fairly new Toyota. Go drop in on
            a writer you met in Vancouver in 1958. Tell each other
            you matter now and you are still the latest thing, and
            it was a good idea after all.

                        ⸻